# TOLERANCE

by Cynthia Roberts

Published in the United States of America by The Child's World®
1980 Lookout Drive • Mankato, MN 56003-1705 • 800-599-READ • www.childsworld.com

The Child's World®: Mary Berendes, Publishing Director; Katherine Stevenson, Editor
The Design Lab: Kathy Petelinsek, Art Director; Julia Goozen, Design and Page Production

Photo Credits: © Alison Wright/Corbis: 9; © Ariel Skelley/Corbis: cover, 17; © Brand X Pictures: 19; © David M. Budd Photography: 11, 15, 21; © Jose Luis Pelaez, Inc./Blend Images/Corbis: 13; © PhotoLink/Getty Images: 7; © Tom Grill/Corbis: 5

Library of Congress Cataloging-in-Publication Data
Roberts, Cynthia, 1960–
  Tolerance / by Cynthia Roberts.
     p. cm. — (Learn about values)
  ISBN 978-1-59296-678-3  ISBN 1-59296-678-0 (library bound : alk. paper)
  1. Tolerance—Juvenile literature. 2. Values—Juvenile literature. I. Title. II. Series.
  BJ1431.R63 2006
  179'.9—dc22                                    2006000969

# CONTENTS

# What Is Tolerance?

People come in all shapes, sizes, and colors. They have different ways of life. They speak all kinds of languages. They wear their hair in different ways. They eat different kinds of foods. They listen to all kinds of music. Tolerance is **accepting** differences in other people. It is thinking, "It is OK that you are different from me!"

Learning from our differences can be fun!

# Tolerance **at School**

Maybe your class is having a **discussion**. The teacher asks all of you to share your ideas. One student has an idea that is different from yours. You show tolerance by listening to the idea. You understand that more than one idea can be **worthwhile**.

We can learn from other people's ideas.

# Tolerance and Your Friends

One of your friends does not speak English well. Everybody around her is talking fast. She does not understand what they are saying. You show tolerance by helping her understand. You explain what they are saying. You do not make fun of her for needing your help.

Differences can make our lives more interesting.

9

# Tolerance on the Playground

Some kids in your class might not have many friends. They might act differently from other kids. On the playground, nobody asks them to play. You can see that they feel left out. You show tolerance by asking them to play. You and your friends make them feel welcome.

Tolerance opens the way to new friendships.

# Tolerance at Home

You and your brother like to watch TV. You like to watch cartoons. Your brother likes nature shows. You show tolerance by letting your brother watch his show. The next day, he shows tolerance by letting you watch cartoons!

Tolerance means accepting that people like to do different things.

# Tolerance in Your Neighborhood

You and your family go to a church in town. You have beliefs about many things. Your neighbors do not go to your church. They have different beliefs from yours. You show tolerance for their ideas. You accept that they believe different things.

Tolerance means respecting other people's beliefs.

15

# Tolerance **and Newcomers**

You have lived in your neighborhood for a long time. One day a new family moves in. They speak and dress differently. They cook different foods. You show tolerance by making them feel welcome. You try to learn about how they do things.

Maybe your new neighbors will become your new friends!

# Tolerance toward Younger Kids

Maybe you have a little sister. She always wants to tag along. She wants to go everywhere you go. She wants to do everything you do. But she is too little to do some things. She does not know as much as you, either. Sometimes she seems like a pest! But you show tolerance by being nice to her. You understand that she is just young.

Being tolerant toward your sister is more fun than being mad!

**19**

# Tolerance Helps Us All Get Along

Showing tolerance makes the world around us much friendlier. If we are tolerant, we can be OK with our differences. We can try to understand one another. We can learn from each other. We can work together. And we can have fun together!

Tolerance makes life more fun!

# glossary

**accept**
When you accept something, you are OK with it.

**discussion**
When people have a discussion, they talk about something.

**worthwhile**
If something is worthwhile, it is useful.

# books

Carolan, Joanna F. *Little World: A Book about Tolerance*. Lawai, HI: Banana Patch Press, 2002.

Copsey, Susan Elizabeth, and Barnabas Kindersley. *Children Just Like Me*. New York: Dorling Kindersley, 1995.

Osborn, Kevin. *Tolerance*. New York: Rosen Publishing, 1993.

# web sites

Visit our Web page for links about character education and values:
*http://www.childsworld.com/links*

Note to parents, teachers, and librarians:
We routinely check our Web links to make sure they're safe, active sites—so encourage your readers to check them out!

# index

# about the author

Even as a child, Cynthia Roberts knew she wanted to be a writer. She is always working to involve kids in reading and writing, and she loves spending time in the children's section of the library or bookstore. Cynthia enjoys gardening, traveling, and having fun with friends and family.